Fortune-Telling with Dice

By Astra Cielo

Copyright © 2020 Lamp of Trismegistus. All rights reserved. No part of this publication may be reproduced or transmitted in any form or by any means, electronic or mechanical, including photocopying, recording, or by any information storage and retrieval system, without permission in writing from Lamp of Trismegistus. Reviewers may quote brief passages.

ISBN: 978-1-63118-466-6

Esoteric Classics

Other Books in this Series and Related Titles

Fortune-Telling by Playing Cards by Astra Cielo (978-1-63118-467-3)

History, Analysis and Secret Tradition of the Tarot
by Manly P. Hall, A. E. Waite &c (978-1-63118-445-1)

Dreams and Their Interpretation by Astra Cielo (978-1-63118-468-0)

Crystal Vision Through Crystal Gazing by Achad (978-1-63118-455-0)

Magical Essays and Instructions by Florence Farr (978-1-63118-418-5)

Ancient Mysteries and Secret Societies by Hall (978-1-63118-410-9)

The Path of Light: A Manual of Maha-Yana Buddhism
by L. D. Barnett (978-1-63118-471-0)

The Rosicrucian Chemical Marriage
by Christian Rosenkreuz (978-1-63118-458-1)

Ghosts in Solid Form by Gambier Bolton (978-1-63118-469-7)

American Indian Freemasonry by A. C. Parker (978-1-63118-460-4)

The Mysteries of Freemasonry & the Druids
by Albert G. Mackey, Manly P. Hall &c (978-1-63118-444-4)

The Legend of the Holy Grail and its Connection with Templars and Freemasons by A. E. Waite (978-1-63118-462-8)

Arcane Formulas or Mental Alchemy
by William Walker Atkinson (978-1-63118-459-8)

The Machinery of the Mind by Dion Fortune (978-1-63118-451-2)

The Gospel of the Nativity of Mary by St. Matthew (978-1-63118-448-2)

Buddhist Psalms by Shinran (978-1-63118-465-9)

Audio Versions are also Available on Audible and iTunes

Table of Contents

Introduction…7

Preface…9

Fortune Telling with Dice…11

Questions…13

Answers…15

INTRODUCTION

The word "esoteric" can be difficult to define. Esotericism in general can be seen less as a system of beliefs and more as a category, which encompasses numerous, different systems of beliefs. It's a bit of juxtaposition, since the word "esoteric" indicates something that few people know about, while the term itself broadly covers numerous philosophies, practices, areas of study and belief systems.

In a greater sense, Esotericism acts as a storehouse for secret knowledge, which is often considered ancient (by *tradition, if not by fact),* passed down from generation to generation, in private. At various times in history, simply possessing the knowledge of some of these subjects, was considered illegal and a jailable offence, if discovered. This usually included such general topics as Alchemy, Qabalah, Hermeticism, Occultism, Ceremonial Magic, Astrology, Divination, Rosicrucianism and so on. Collectively, these areas of study were often referred to as the esoteric sciences.

Sometimes, the outer garment of a subject isn't esoteric, while what is hidden beneath it, is. As an example, Freemasonry isn't necessarily esoteric by nature (at *least not anymore),* but certain signs, passwords and handshakes given to the candidate during their initiation, are in fact, esoteric, in the sense that they are hidden from the general public.

Today, in the twenty-first century, such topics are readily available at bookstores across the country, and numerous mainsteam publishers offer beginners guides and coffee-table volumes on many of these subjects, intended for mass appeal. Books like *"The Secret"* have turned previously arcane topics into household knowledge. All that being the case, however, it isn't to say that there still aren't buried secrets to uncover, ancient wisdom being ignored and forgotten mysteries to be explored. In fact, it is often that we are only able to further our own studies by standing on the shoulders of these disappearing giants.

Lamp of Trismegistus is doing its part to help preserve humanity's esoteric history by making some of these classics available to those students who are seeking to unearth the knowledge of these ancient colossi.

So, be sure to check other titles from our *Esoteric Classics* series, as well as our *Occult Fiction*, *Theosophical Classics*, *Foundations of Freemasonry Series*, *Supernatural Fiction*, *Paranormal Research Series*, *Studies in Buddhism* and our *Christian Apocrypha Series*. You can also download the audio versions of most of these titles from iTunes or Audible, for learning on the go.

PREFACE

This work was written during the early twentieth century and is detailing a style of divination that was much earlier, still. During this time period, it wasn't uncommon for fortune-tellers using this type of table-top divination, to favor women customers. It is from such trends that we get clichéd scenes of gypsy fortune-tellers telling a young female client about a tall, dark, handsome stranger who will enter into her life soon, usually with motives of romance. In a similar fashion, the reader will notice that many of the questions posed in this book, seem to be catered toward women and specifically focused on queries of love.

In an attempt to use this small book in a modern era, I will make a few recommendations.

Firstly, in the instance of love, it's perfectly reasonable to simply make any necessary adjustments, such as a man asking about a woman (instead of a woman asking about a man) or a woman asking about another woman or a man asking about another man and so forth.

Secondly, any professional fortune-teller will tell you that there are only a handful of subjects that clients primarily ask about. Love certainly tops that list, usually followed by money, employment (which is related to money) and health. This book, due to its age, seems to be functioning under the premise that the woman in question will likely never be seeking a job (since it doesn't outright appear on the list); however, several questions can potentially be re-interpreted as to be about a potential employer. Or, the question about travel could be work-related; the same goes with receiving a letter. Use your imagination and be creative with interpretations.

If your question is one which doesn't appear on the list, you should make an attempt to choose a question with a similar broad intention. And, from that, you may also need to creatively interpret the answer, while staying within the same frame of mind.

Thirdly, if the result of your query isn't what you were hoping for or the answer doesn't seem to align with your modern question, rather than re-rolling for a secondary answer, try asking one or two different (but related) questions and then combining all of the answers, when you're finished, for an overall and broader view of the situation.

And finally, if this outdated style of divination doesn't seem to be working for you, it's perfectly acceptable to treat it as more of a parlor game between friends, than as an oracle.

FORTUNE-TELLING WITH DICE

A very ancient and fascinating way of telling one's fortune is by means of two dice, and the following tables make the game easy and interesting. We have confined ourselves to twenty questions, comprising those which would most naturally occur to inquirers desiring to know the future.

Two dice are used. The inquirer first selects the question to be answered, and calling this question aloud, takes the dice either in his palms or in a cup, and throws them on the table. The number of spots of the upper surface of the dice are noted, the corresponding table of answers is consulted, and the answer corresponds in number to the question asked.

If, for example, a lady has chosen the question 5, "How many beaux shall I have?" and the dice fall with numbers 2 and 3 facing upward, the answer would be, "Perhaps one, possibly none." The same plan is adopted with dominoes, except that all stones containing blanks must first be thrown out. The dominoes are laid with the backs upward, mixed thoroughly, and one at a time selected, and turned over. The number of spots indicate which table of answers is to be consulted.

QUESTIONS

01. Does he ever think of me?
02. Will someone soon pay me attention?
03. What must I do to please him?
04. Shall I do what is asked of me?
05. How many beaux shall I have?
06. What kind of a man will my husband be?
07. May I trust him?
08. Does he love me?
09. Shall I get married soon?
10. Shall I have many adventures?
11. Shall I be wealthy?
12. Will my secret be discovered?
13. What do people think of me?
14. Shall I see him soon?
15. Shall I receive a letter soon?
16. Shall I receive a present soon?
17. Shall I take a journey soon?
18. Will my condition be improved?
19. Will my wish be fulfilled?
20. Will it prove a blessing?

ANSWERS

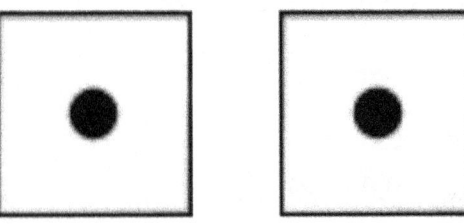

01. He has too much to think about for such thoughts.

02. If you would treat a certain gentleman with a little more regard, he would appreciate it.

03. Do not receive the attention of others.

04. Say what your heart dictates.

05. One, a stout and very unpoetical fellow.

06. Very tall, dark complexioned, quarrelsome, of a jealous disposition; rough, but with the best intentions.

07. Find out what people say about him. It is rumored that there is much falsehood in him.

08. With his heart and soul.

09. In five months or more.

10. No, very few, indeed.

11. You will have money, but you must bear in mind that money does not always make one rich, nor give happiness, and sometimes is the source of bitter woe.

12. If you tell it to nobody; otherwise not.

13. A genius in every respect, but for that reason you are thought to have a great many faults.

14. At an unexpected time.

15. Yes, for it will make you very happy.

16. Not very soon.

17. Yes, the journey of which you are thinking at present.

18. Not in the way you would like it.

19. Yes, sooner than expected.

20. Yes, although at first you will not be aware of it.

 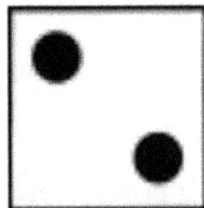

01. Very often; as often as circumstances permit.

02. Wrinkles will be visible on you before that happens.

03. Do not be so terribly affected. Show him by your manners that you have a heart and are honest and sensible.

04. Be careful, for you might be laughed at.

05. One, a very good and amiable young man.

06. Amiable, cheerful, a little romantic, somewhat poetical, good-hearted, but weak.

07. Look in his open, honest countenance and you will know.

08. Simply with ordinary brotherly affection, nothing more.

09. Four years from now.

10. Your life will be rather wearisome.

11. If you are painstaking and very economical.

12. There is one person who knows it, but will never disclose it.

13. A mere fashionable puppet, heartless and soulless.

14. Yes, rather soon.

15. Yes, bringing sad news.

16. Be patient for some time.

17. Not quite as soon as desired.

18. Very soon, and in an unforeseen way.

19. Yes, but not completely, and not quite as desired.

20. If it is taken as Fortune means it.

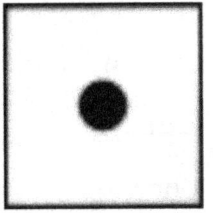 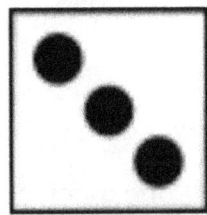

01. You know exactly what he does.

02. Yes, but only to make a fool out of you.

03. Do not use too much sugar in your coffee, or he will think you extravagant.

04. Yes, do it, if it can be done without blushing.

05. Three, and not one good for much.

06. A little conceited, vain fellow with rather a heavy mustache.

07. Be prudent.

08. Yes, but you share his heart with other admirers.

09. No matter how hard you try, it will not be sooner than four years.

10. Many, but not interesting ones.

11. You will have more than a competence; but you will lose heavily if you or your husband play at cards with money.

12. You will disclose it.

13. Quick at repartee, but not really witty.

14. Not so soon, you will have to wait a while.

15. Yes, quite a long one.

16. Very soon, and which will give you much pleasure.

17. Yes, but it will cost you many tears.

18. Soon, by an unexpected occurrence.

19. It will, more fully than expected.

20. It will cost you many tears at first, but will end happily.

 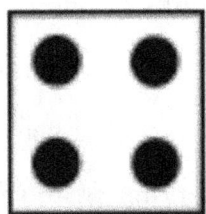

01. He is thinking of you now, very lovingly and seriously.

02. Yes, many, and three at the same time.

03. Dress your hair neatly, do not wink, sit up erect and be very cordial to everybody.

04. What will a particular person say about it, if you do?

05. Two, a foolish old fellow, and a wild young man.

06. A man of strong character, energetic and haughty, with wit and humor.

07. He deserves much confidence.

08. He is merely a true friend to you; no more.

09. Yes, very soon.

10. Very many interesting ones.

11. If you do not speculate.

12. If you keep it a secret; but you gossip too much.

13. Very peculiar, by some. There is one person who understands you.

14. Not until you are both gray.

15. Not soon, but then it will be a very tender conclusion.

16. No one thinks of giving you anything, just now.

17. Yes, and it will give you much pleasure.

18. Soon, and in such a way that seemed to you impossible.

19. Yes, but very far from the present.

20. If you are thoughtful, cheerful, and try to be an optimist.

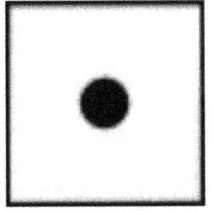 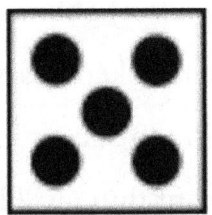

01. He does think of you, for which you will be sorry someday.

02. No, not for a long time.

03. Do not be sentimental, but show common sense in whatever you say and do.

04. Yes, for he will ask nothing of which you may fear.

05. Three very fine and intelligent gentlemen.

06. A very big-built gentleman, and very conceited.

07. Hear what your best and dearest friends have to say about it.

08. No. He loves another.

09. When you love a particular person more than you do now.

10. Yes, but you will tire of them.

11. You will have money, and if you use it to good advantage it will last, otherwise not.

12. Yes, it will.

13. Haughty, conceited and discreet.

14. Yes, but not very soon.

15. Yes, from a broken heart.

16. Yes, but do not accept it.

17. An important thing will happen which will prevent it, it will bring joy to you.

18. Yes, but a long time from now.

19. Your wish will be fulfilled if you take care as to how you act.

20. Yes, if you are cautious.

 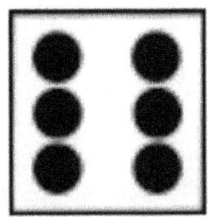

01. He thinks of you very often.

02. Yes, but it will not bring you happiness.

03. Always be happy and pleasant; never be angry.

04. Your mother's advice is best.

05. None.

06. A young, handsome man who loves you very much.

07. Take the advice of an older female friend.

08. His was love at first sight, and lasting.

09. You will soon fall in love, perhaps on your next journey.

10. A few interesting ones, and you will be protected against the unpleasant ones.

11. Yes, but not very.

12. Everybody seems to be unconcerned about it.

13. People think well of you.

14. He is thinking of coming to you soon.

15. Yes, you will soon receive an interesting one.

16. A little pleasing present, not so soon.

17. You will not take advantage of an opportunity.

18. Yes, and to your advantage.

19. It is up to yourself.

20. Yes, and it will make you very happy.

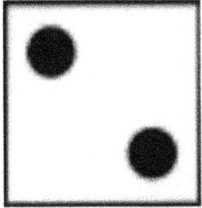 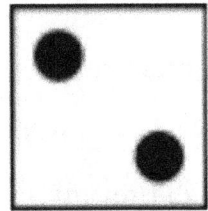

01. He thinks of you, but not very seriously.

02. You will have many charming ones.

03. Try to have your skin tanned, by means of the sun.

04. To a certain extent.

05. Twenty-five, if you take advantage of all offers.

06. Ugly, lame, and very thin and tall.

07. Yes, by all means.

08. He loves you, but conceals it because he does not think it is reciprocated.

09. Within two years.

10. No, very few.

11. You will be wealthy as you wish.

12. Guard yourself and others, for there has been a leak.

13. Good at heart, but conceited and not very sensible.

14. Perhaps thru some coincidence, for he has sworn never to call.

15. You will receive rather a mysterious one.

16. Yes, a very small and dear one.

17. Some sad interference will prevent it for some time.

18. Yes, but not as you wish it.

19. Enemies will prevent it.

20. Pleasure at first, but later will cause tears.

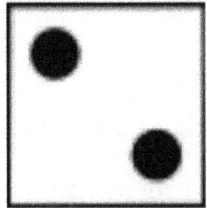 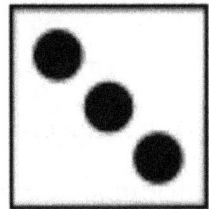

01. He is thinking tenderly of you at this moment.

02. A fellow of a very stout appearance.

03. Pay very much attention to him, sit at his left side and eat nothing that contains onions.

04. No, let him coax for a while.

05. Perhaps one, possibly none.

06. Beloved of all, favorite in society and among ladies, and a darling of yours above all.

07. Yes, by all means, for he never deceived you.

08. Yes, but it is very painful to him.

09. In two years or more.

10. Quite some.

11. Be satisfied with what you have.

12. Some know it already.

13. Original and witty.

14. In a month and two days.

15. Yes, this week.

16. Yes, but you will be sorry that you ever got it.

17. Yes, and with a gentleman.

18. Yes, and it will bring joy to you.

19. Something will interfere and delay its fulfillment.

20. If you overcome all anxieties on its account, it will.

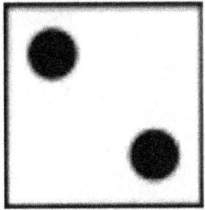 

01. Very little, but still it is more than you think of him.

02. Yes, a romantic, sentimental, foolish fellow.

03. You must learn table etiquette.

04. It would bring joy to you, but sorrow to more than one.

05. One, and he will be a burden to you.

06. A weak-minded drunkard and gambler.

07. Yes, but be watchful.

08. He loves you as much as you allow him to, which is not very much.

09. In four or five years.

10. They will be mischievous ones, and cause trouble.

11. Yes, very; in ten years.

12. Be cautious, and it will not.

13. At times foolish, but prudent and quite humorous and witty.

14. Next spring, when the snow melts.

15. The one wished for is on its way.

16. Yes, and you will rejoice over it.

17. No, but perhaps a year from now.

18. Yes, as you wish it.

19. It will, but not so soon.

20. It will prove as you interpret it.

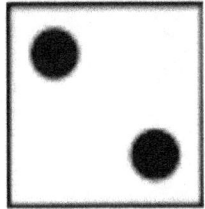 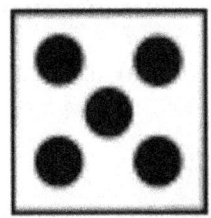

01. He very seldom thinks of anything or anybody.

02. Tomorrow a person will fall in love with you.

03. Try to be as witty as possible.

04. Take your father's advice.

05. Three worthy gentlemen, within a month.

06. Handsome and well situated in the business world.

07. Trust him as far as you feel it is safe.

08. He would love you if he knew it would be mutual.

09. In three years.

10. Some at intervals of years.

11. You will have plenty if economical.

12. No, but would be to your advantage to have it discovered.

13. Humorous and interesting.

14. At the next meeting of a large crowd.

15. Do not expect one very soon, for he is very angry.

16. Yes, and from one you love dearly.

17. Not soon, but then it will bring much pleasure to you.

18. According to how you act. Be cautious.

19. Yes, but to your disadvantage.

20. If it happens naturally, it will bring joy.

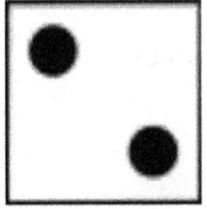 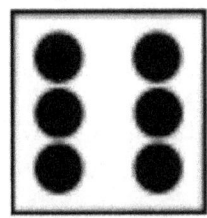

01. Very little.

02. Yes, from a soldier.

03. Please him in every respect.

04. It would do no harm if you would.

05. One, and he will give himself entirely up to you.

06. A fellow who will be a burden to you.

07. He is fond of flirting, but is true to you.

08. He loves you only.

09. In four or five years.

10. Only while out of your hometown.

11. If you are economical.

12. It may, but a long time from now.

13. Clear understanding, but a very poor listener.

14. Today perhaps.

15. No, unless it is an answer to yours.

16. Yes, but from one you don't admire.

17. There will be no particular opportunity, but perhaps you will.

18. Yes, but not so soon.

19. Yes, but it will bring sorrow to someone.

20. No, unfortunately not.

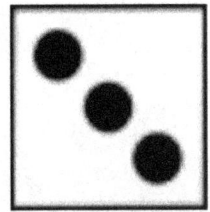 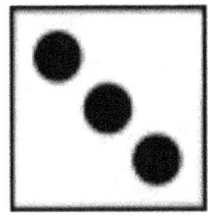

01. He is constantly thinking of you.

02. Not in two or three years yet.

03. Be patient, and allow him to have his own way.

04. If you do, you may regret it.

05. One, but an unworthy one.

06. Very uninteresting and tiresome.

07. You would hurt his feelings, if you did not.

08. Very much, and very dearly.

09. In five years.

10. Only when you attend crowds of people.

11. Conveniently so.

12. Not so soon. Be cautious.

13. Just so. You have many admirers.

14. Be independent and wait for him to come, before going to him.

15. No, not a present.

16. Yes, but not a very large one.

17. As you desire; it will be up to yourself.

18. Not that it will make much of a difference.

19. Yes, and it will bring many friends to you.

20. Yes, in disguise.

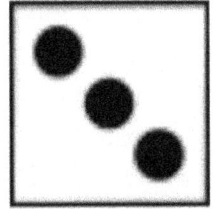 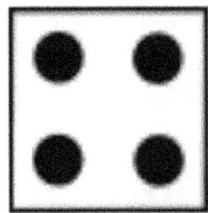

01. Yes, very pleasing thoughts.

02. Yes, very many and at the present time.

03. When you see him again, place a flower in his buttonhole.

04. Do it unintentionally.

05. Four at the same time.

06. Disfigured and very ugly, but you will not notice it.

07. Do not trust him, unless you feel sure that he can be trusted.

08. He cannot live without you.

09. In six or seven years.

10. Many at unexpected times.

11. For a very short time only.

12. Yes, but not so soon.

13. All think you very witty and humorous, but conceited.

14. He will not come; laboring under a wrong impression.

15. Yes, a very interesting one.

16. No, not for a long while.

17. A very short one.

18. When you most heartily wish for it.

19. Yes, but that will bring you an enemy which will sadden the joy.

20. A blessing to all.

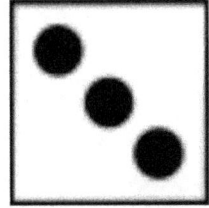 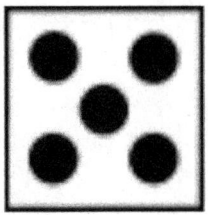

01. He thinks as often of you as you of him.

02. Tomorrow evening about 8 o'clock.

03. Answer, but do it gracefully.

04. No, you must not do it.

05. Only one.

06. Pleasant and handsome.

07. No. He is a scoundrel.

08. He feels that he cannot help himself.

09. In a week or more.

10. Your life will be very peaceful.

11. You will always have plenty.

12. It would be very good to be discovered.

13. Not witty, and interesting only at times.

14. Yes, very soon.

15. Tomorrow perhaps.

16. Not so soon as you desire.

17. Very soon, along one.

18. Yes, to your happiness.

19. It will not.

20. Yes, to the best happiness.

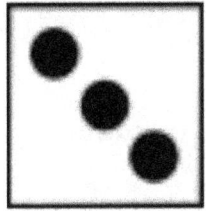 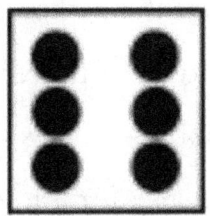

01. He does not.

02. Unfortunately for you, much too soon.

03. He hates to see you dressed with a low-necked dress and bare arms.

04. Yes, without any fear.

05. Two; one squints, and the other is bald.

06. Tall and round. He is patient and fond of sweet things.

07. You have had enough proofs that he has the best heart in the world.

08. He is yours in heart and soul.

09. In three years.

10. Your life will be like a foaming torrent.

11. As wealthy as you are at present.

12. No, but is advisable to disclose it quickly.

13. Neither very discreet nor very witty, very interesting to one.

14. Before the autumn wind blows over the meadow.

15. Yes, but not the wished-for one.

16. Yes, a bouquet of flowers.

17. You will soon see cities which you never expected to visit.

18. When you wish for it to change.

19. If that is really your wish.

20. No. That is an impossibility at present.

01. He thinks of you in sleep and in dreams.

02. You are constantly surrounded by admirers.

03. Treat him with frankness and candor, but don't act coquettishly.

04. Whatever you do, do it prudently.

05. One, and a very jealous one who will constantly watch you.

06. Loving and tender; he will claim daily a score of kisses.

07. Always; you need not mistrust him so very much.

08. Does not his pale countenance betray his deep sorrow?

09. Yes, in six weeks or more.

10. Yes, thrilling adventures.

11. Quite rich.

12. It will unless you guard yourself cautiously.

13. A good creature.

14. No. You are separated forever.

15. Yes, one is now on its way.

16. Yes, but not from the one you expect.

17. A short, sentimental one.

18. Yes, but it will not be of much advantage to you.

19. If you do your, best to promote it.

20. It will bring both joy and sorrow.

 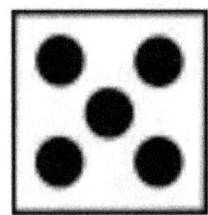

01. Your eyes are a pair of stars which, once seen, can never be forgotten.
02. Yes, but be prudent, for he is a sad rogue.
03. Show more kindness to human beings, and less toward cats.
04. It would be unjust to refuse.
05. One; a fat little fellow.
06. Very ugly, but in your eyes the very handsomest.
07. Yes, with your full heart.
08. Do you not see his cheeks redden when he looks at you?
09. Never, or not till late in life.
10. Too many, especially love adventures.
11. Your wealth will exceed your knowledge of what to do with it.
12. It is discovered at the present time.
13. A mischievous little vixen.
14. Very soon, sooner than you expect.
15. The one you want you will never receive.

16. Very soon, a very sweet one.

17. Yes, the one you are looking forward to with pleasure.

18. It will depend upon yourself only.

19. Yes, certainly.

20. It will bring joy and happiness to you.

 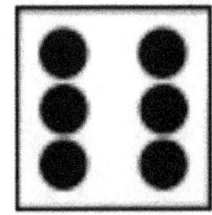

01. He would like to, but is afraid.

02. When you cease your coquettish ways.

03. Upon your next meeting, give him your hand and say, "I am exceedingly happy to call you my friend."

04. You cannot well do anything else.

05. One, and he will bring much joy into your life.

06. Very tall, brown-complexioned, noble, manly and amiable young man who wears spectacles.

07. You may believe him and not the world's tittle-tattle.

08. The next time you hand him a glass of water, and if in taking it he tries to touch your hand, he loves you.

09. In a year and six months.

10. Very many with rogues and robbers.

11. Rich in love and all amiable virtues, but not rich in money.

12. You think it to be a secret, but it never has been one.

13. Very capricious.

14. If you write that he should come, otherwise not.

15. Very soon, and a very tender one.

16. Yes, a living present, with a kiss.

17. Yes, but not the one you are now thinking of.

18. Not very soon.

19. Yes, but not so soon as you would like it.

20. As long as you keep your heart pure and true.

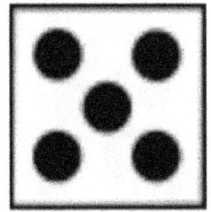 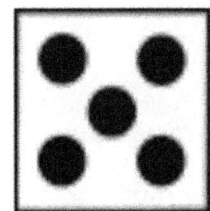

01. He tries not to, for when he does it is very painful.

02. A rich old, lame gentleman, with a mustache.

03. Do not conceal your love; prove it by sending him a gift.

04. It will bring about important consequences, depending upon yourself whether it will be advantageous or not.

05. It is best that you have none.

06. A very handsome man, a genius, and your love is mutual.

07. Trust him and him only.

08. In the same way as you love him.

09. When the first snow falls.

10. You are subject to many.

11. Your present conditions will continue.

12. Yes, by an enemy who will betray it.

13. Very artless, nothing else.

14. At the beginning of autumn.

15. In a month or so, the longed-for one.

16. Someone is thinking at present to make you one, but whether he will or not is unknown.

17. Yes, to England.

18. Yes, soon.

19. To a very small extent.

20. It will bring much happiness to you.

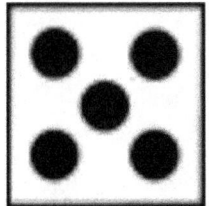 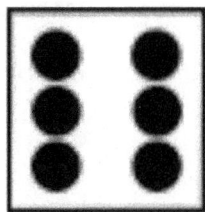

01. No, perhaps later.
02. One is paying attention to you at the present time.
03. He thinks you faultless.
04. If you think it will give you pleasure and joy.
05. One, the one you love.
06. A witty fellow, full of mischief and fun.
07. Take care in trusting him.
08. He does, but conceals it.
09. This year or next.
10. A very interesting one, but not so soon.
11. Yes, but be very economical.
12. Yes, next week all will be known.
13. Very silly at times, but you are pardoned by all.
14. You have driven him away, he will never return.
15. This week; a very interesting one.
16. Perhaps this week, but surely this month.
17. Yes, to some other foreign country.
18. To some extent, and will bring much joy.

19. It is up to your behavior.

20. It will bring many happy hours.

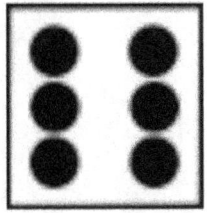 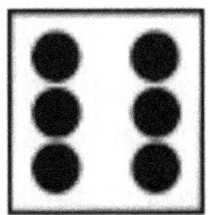

01. Yes, but with sorrow.

02. Yes, it will start by the presentation of a flower.

03. Whatever you do will not please him. He is a faultfinder.

04. If you do, you will be laughed at by the one of whom you are asked to do it.

05. One, an unexpected one.

06. A worthless fellow who will bring you sorrow, yet a dear fellow.

07. Don't place too much confidence in him.

08. He loves you very much and would be happy to gain your hand.

09. Next spring.

10. Not very soon, but you will in time.

11. If you make up your mind to be.

12. Yes, when least expected.

13. Very foolish at times, yet witty at other times.

14. Tomorrow perhaps.

15. Yes, sooner than you expect.

16. Yes, a ring.

17. A pleasant trip eastward.

18. Not the way that you would wish it.

19. If you desire it truthfully.

20. At present it is doubtful.

www.ingramcontent.com/pod-product-compliance
Lightning Source LLC
LaVergne TN
LVHW041459070426
835507LV00009B/694